Inspection of U.S. Customs and Border Protection Miami Field Office Ports of Entry

December 18, 2014

Why We Did This

U.S. Customs and Border Protection's (CBP) Office of Field Operations is responsible for port of entry operations. It enforces antiterrorism regulations, trade laws, immigration policy, and agricultural laws and regulations at 328 ports of entry. The ports of entry include airports, seaports, and designated land border crossings. The Miami Field Office encompasses five ports that span 313 miles of Florida coastline, within which there are five seaports, including the top two cruise ship ports in the world. In addition, there are nine airports, with Miami International Airport ranking as the second busiest international U.S. airport and the largest air cargo port for international freight among U.S. airports. We conducted this review to determine whether CBP Miami Field Office ports of entry operations comply with CBP policies and procedures.

What We Recommend

To assist Miami Field Office ports of entry operations, we made four recommendations, which, when implemented, should improve passenger screening, agriculture safeguarding operations, and cargo targeting.

For Further Information:
Contact our Office of Public Affairs at (202) 254-4100, or email us at
DHS-OIG.OfficePublicAffairs@oig.dhs.gov

What We Found

In most instances, the CBP Miami Field Office complied with CBP policies and procedures. We found only minor deficiencies in CBP Miami Field Office operations for cargo targeting and seized asset management. For passenger screening, Miami International Airport leveraged an existing system to track passengers who have records for violations of laws or other significant events. Other Miami Field Office ports of entry could benefit from this "one-stop system" that would allow them to document, monitor, and report on targeting passengers in real time. The field office could improve the consistency of its recordkeeping for changes to the biometric watchlist. Also, the CBP Miami Field Office needs to improve its compliance with safeguards for using high security bolt seals during cargo screening. Lastly, the CBP Miami Field Office needs to update its policy and procedures for agriculture inspections so they align with current U.S. Department of Agriculture procedures.

CBP Response

CBP concurred with all of our recommendations.

Table of Contents

Results of Inspection 1

Background 1

    Passenger Analytical Units 2
    Biometric Watchlist Changes 2
    High Security Bolt Seals 3
    Agriculture Screening Policies and Procedures 4
    Other Issues Observed at CBP Miami Field Office Ports of Entry 5

Recommendations 6

Appendixes

Appendix A: Transmittal to Action Official 9
Appendix B: Scope and Methodology 10
Appendix C: CBP Comments to the Draft Report 15
Appendix D: Major Contributors to This Report 17
Appendix E: Report Distribution 18

Abbreviations

AQAS	Agriculture Quarantine Activity Systems
ATU	Advance Targeting Unit
CBP	U.S. Customs and Border Protection
DHS	Department of Homeland Security
EAN	Emergency Action Notification
FY	fiscal year
MIA	Miami International Airport
OIG	Office of Inspector General
USDA	U.S. Department of Agriculture

Results of Inspection

In most instances, the CBP Miami Field Office complied with CBP policies and procedures. We found only minor deficiencies in CBP Miami Field Office operations for cargo targeting and seized asset management. For passenger screening, Miami International Airport leveraged an existing system to track passengers who have records for violations of laws or for other significant events. Other Miami Field Office ports of entry could benefit from this "one-stop system" that would allow them to document, monitor, and report on targeting passengers in real time. The field office could improve the consistency of its recordkeeping for changes to the biometric watchlist. Also, the CBP Miami Field Office needs to improve its compliance with safeguards for using bolt seals during cargo screening. Lastly, the CBP Miami Field Office needs to update its policy and procedures for agriculture inspections to be in line with current U.S. Department of Agriculture (USDA) procedures.

Background

CBP has a complex mission to protect the Nation against cross-border violations. The Office of Field Operations enforces antiterrorism regulations, trade laws, immigration policy, and agricultural laws and regulations at 328 ports of entry, which include airports, seaports, and designated land border crossings. The Miami Field Office encompasses five ports that span 313 miles of Florida coastline, within which there are five seaports, including the top two cruise ship ports in the world. In addition, there are nine airports, with Miami International Airport (MIA) ranking as the second busiest international U.S. airport and the largest air cargo port for international freight among U.S. airports.

We reviewed three Miami Field Office ports of entry—MIA, Miami Seaport, and Port Everglades (air and sea). At these ports of entry, we reviewed six areas within passenger screening, cargo inspection, and agriculture operations; and seized asset management to determine compliance with policies and procedures. Specifically, we reviewed:

- Passenger Analytical Units
- Biometric Watchlist
- Cargo Targeting
- High Security Bolt Seals[1]
- Pest Exclusion for Cut Flowers
- Seized Asset Management

---

[1] Port Everglades and the Miami Seaport have two offices that use bolt seals. After opening a container for inspection or other purposes, CBP officers secure the container with a standardized high-security bolt seal to preserve the integrity of the container leaving CBP's possession and to prevent refusal of delivery and unnecessary delay in allowing legitimate cargo to enter U.S. commerce.

We conducted this review to determine whether CBP Miami Field Office ports of entry operations comply with CBP policies and procedures.

Passenger Analytical Units

Passenger screening operations at CBP's Miami Field Office's ports involve multiple systems that do not interface, which inhibits documentation, monitoring, and reporting of information related to passenger screening. However, by leveraging an existing asset, MIA has created a "one-stop" system that allows CBP officers to document, monitor, and report passenger screening information in real time. Implementing such a system at the Miami Field Office's other ports would improve the effectiveness of their passenger screening operations.

Miami Field Office's Passenger Analytical Units analyze, target, and incorporate intelligence information and technology to determine whether CBP needs to further inspect inbound and outbound passengers. Using multiple systems to gather information on passengers is labor intensive. In fiscal year (FY) 2014, MIA leveraged the capabilities of an existing system, the Targeting Framework, which tracks passengers who have records for violations of laws or for other significant events. By leveraging the Targeting Framework's capabilities, MIA created a one-stop system. At the time of our review, MIA was piloting the system.

The Targeting Framework is available to all ports of entry nationwide, but according to CBP, each port has unique needs when tracking targeted individuals from initial identification to final disposition. Thus, although MIA is able to use the Targeting Framework effectively as a one-stop system, other ports may not be able to do so. Without a system to document, monitor, and report passenger screening information in real time, the CBP Miami Field Office ports may fail to identify systemic issues that require national attention.

Biometric Watchlist Changes

DHS maintains a biometric watchlist (watchlist) of potential terrorists, criminals, immigration violators, and other persons of interest based on the existence of derogatory information. In biometrics, an electronic device or system detects and records a person's unique physical and other traits, such as fingerprints, to confirm identity. This information is used to develop a biometric watchlist, which is obtained from various Federal organizations and is used to identify potential terrorists, criminals, immigration violators, or other persons of interest. Individuals are promoted (added) to or demoted (removed) from the watchlist based on available information.

The CBP Miami Field Office did not maintain all documentation on individuals who had overcome their immigration inadmissibility issues and were removed from the watchlist from FYs 2011–13. Port Everglades officials did not maintain all documentation for FYs 2011–12. Additionally, CBP officials said, "Headquarters does not maintain the information on removals." Because there was no written requirement to maintain documentation or data on those removed from the watchlist in previous years, there is no assurance that individuals who were removed should have been removed. It is important to maintain the data because it provides a record to ensure that individuals were properly removed from the watchlist.

High Security Bolt Seals

We identified instances of noncompliance with Miami Field Office's policy for high security bolt seals (bolt seals). CBP officers use bolt seals to secure cargo containers that have been opened for inspection or other purposes. Our review showed that 63 percent of the records we reviewed for bolt seals showed instances of noncompliance with CBP's policies and procedures. (See appendix B for information on our methodology.) We found:

- files missing bolt serial numbers;
- files missing the names of officers and supervisors required to document changes in custody;
- bolt seal serial numbers were missing from CBP's Cargo Enforcement Reporting and Tracking System; and
- instances in which Miami Seaport supervisors signed out bolt seals to themselves.

Bolt seal policy contributes to the integrity of bolt seal usage. Adherence to policy ensures the security and integrity of the cargo. The quality and integrity of the seal is critical to preventing use of cargo containers to import illicit materials and contraband, including Weapons of Mass Destruction and other terrorist devices, into the United States.

At Port Everglades and Miami Seaport, 32 of 384 files were missing bolt seal serial numbers. Of the 32, 24 were in CBP supervisory inventory logs and 8 were in CBP officer inventory logs. According to *CBP's Seal Standards*, each port must maintain CBP officer and CBP supervisory inventory logs with serial numbers as a mandatory field. In response to our finding, the Miami Field Office, on August 3, 2014, reiterated the requirement to its ports to maintain inventory log book documentation for bolt seals at ports of entry.

In 206 of 384 files, neither the CBP officer nor the CBP supervisor name/signature were on the log, as required to document bolt seals changing custody. This occurred because the Miami Field Office does not have a standardized format for log books. The Miami Seaport and Port Everglades offices using bolt seals created their own supervisory log book formats, but some offices did not include the mandatory field for the supervisor's name/signature. In response to our finding, the Miami Field Office created standardized log books for both CBP supervisors and CBP officers with mandatory fields as specified in *CBP's Seal Standards*. As of August 2014, the new log books are in use at all the Miami Field Office ports of entry.

Additionally, in two instances, CBP Miami Seaport supervisors signed out bolt seals to themselves. According to the *CBP's Seal Standards*, CBP supervisory logs must have a supervisor signing out bolt seals to a CBP officer. According to CBP officials, having both signatures for issuing bolt seals is not always feasible, especially in tight timeframes and situations with limited staff. Without proper accountability for the inventory of bolt seals at each port, there may be errors, misuse, or fraud. For example, bolt seals could be used on containers with dangerous weapons or illicit contraband and allowed to enter a U.S. port of entry without inspection. Based on our finding, the Miami Field Office issued a memorandum requiring CBP supervisors to follow additional oversight and approval procedures to mitigate risk when a CBP supervisor cannot issue a bolt seal to a CBP officer.

We also identified 34 of 384 instances in which the bolt seal serial number was missing in CBP's Cargo Enforcement Reporting and Tracking System. According to the *Cargo Enforcement Reporting and Tracking System Port Guidance*, after completing a cargo inspection, bolt seal serial numbers must be recorded in the system to preserve the integrity of the cargo in inspected containers. Miami Seaport and Port Everglades officials believed that staff data entry errors caused the majority of missing serial numbers for inbound containers in the system. In response to the missing bolt seal serial numbers, the Miami Field Office, on August 3, 2014, reiterated the requirement for CBP officials to record bolt seal information accurately in CBP's targeting system following an inspection.

Agriculture Screening Policies and Procedures

Figure 1. Photo of MIA CBP Agriculture Specialist Examining Cut Flowers for Pests.

Agriculture Safeguarding

The agriculture industry is the largest industry and employment sector in the United States, with more than $1 trillion in annual economic activity. One of the biggest risks to this industry is pests. It is crucial that CBP prevent prohibited pests, which can be detrimental to our agriculture system, from entering the United States. Invasive species cause $136 billion annually in lost agriculture revenue. At MIA, Agriculture Operations inspects cargo to prevent prohibited animal, plant, and food products from entering the United States. Cut flowers at MIA constitute 75 percent of agriculture inspections.

Pest Exclusion for Cut Flowers

MIA's policies and procedures for making referrals and safeguarding shipments containing pests in cut flowers do not reflect the current process. MIA makes referrals to USDA to identify pests found in cut flowers shipments. CBP MIA uses *USDA's Manual for Agriculture Clearance* and *USDA's Emergency Action Notification (EAN) v2.0 Policy Guide* (EAN policy guide). The Manual for Agriculture Clearance includes guidance for referrals and for safeguarding shipments; the EAN policy guide provides specific guidance on information that should be entered into USDA's Agriculture Quarantine Activity Systems (AQAS).

MIA's standard operating procedures include an outdated manual process of using a CBP referral log. CBP's local policy also mandates issuing an EAN form from AQAS to include the complete master and house air waybill numbers. CBP agriculture specialists are also required to include complete address and phone numbers of the owner, consignee, of the commodity. Because all information should now be captured in AQAS, the manual referral log is no longer used. Additionally, USDA's EAN policy guide does not mandate including phone numbers of the owner of the commodity. The EAN policy guide requires the bill of lading and shipper's name and address as mandatory fields.

According to MIA's agriculture cargo safeguarding procedures, specified actions, such as fumigation of a commodity, must be completed in 24 hours. According to MIA officials, the 24-hour period is not the timeframe for treating the cargo but the time given to the shipper or importer to notify MIA of the chosen action for the cargo. MIA's policy does not clearly define this 24-hour requirement to ensure compliance with policy.

Without current policies or procedures for safeguarding agriculture cargo, MIA cannot ensure that all CBP officers follow USDA's requirements, and management may not be able to detect and respond to issues of noncompliance.

Other Issues Observed at CBP Miami Field Office Ports of Entry

National Sea Cargo Targeting Training

According to the *National Maritime Targeting Policy*, CBP employees assigned to the Advance Targeting Unit (ATU) must attend the National Sea Cargo Targeting Training course as soon as practicable, but no later than 2 years after their assignment to the ATU. Although ATU employees at Miami Seaport and Port Everglades complied with training requirements, there is no refresher training. Of the 31 personnel at CBP Miami Seaport and Port Everglades from FYs 2011 to 2013, 15, or 48 percent, of ATU employees completed the course more than 5 years ago. Of the 15 employees, 4 completed the training more than 9 years ago, and 1 as far back as 2003. According to CBP officials, it would not be cost effective to develop a refresher training course, but job aids and musters could be used to provide needed refresher training.

Recommendations

Recommendation 1. We recommend that the CBP Miami Field Office, Director of Field Operations: Share the best practices of MIA's use of the Targeting Framework and allow ports to use those aspects that may be most beneficial to their unique operational needs to document, monitor and report passenger screening operations effectively.

Recommendation 2. We recommend that the CBP Assistant Commissioner, Office of Field Operations: Develop a retention policy for documentation when removing individuals from the biometric watchlist.

Recommendation 3. We recommend that the CBP Miami Field Office, Director of Field Operations: Review and update policies and procedures for cargo shipments referred to USDA and for agriculture cargo safeguarding to properly reflect current practices and procedures.

Recommendation 4. We recommend that the CBP Miami Field Office, Director of Field Operations: Develop job aids and hold musters as refresher training for ATU employees.

CBP Comments

CBP provided comments on the draft of this report. A copy of the response in its entirety is included in appendix C. CBP also provided technical comments and suggested revisions to our report in a separate document. We reviewed CBP's technical comments and made changes throughout our report where appropriate.

OIG Analysis of CBP Comments

Management Comments to Recommendation #1
Concur. According to CBP, it already has systems in place that are used to document, monitor, and report on passenger screening operations. MIA uses the Targeting Framework, as an additional tool. The Miami Field Office will share the best practices of MIA's use of the Targeting Framework and allow ports to use those aspects which may be most beneficial to their unique operational needs. The Miami Field Office will promote the best practices of the

existing Targeting Framework capabilities for ports to adapt based on their operational requirements. The estimated completion date is January 31, 2015.

OIG Analysis

Although CBP has systems to document, monitor, and report on passenger screening operations, the multiple systems do not interface, and they inhibit documentation, monitoring, and reporting. MIA's use of the Targeting Framework as a "one-stop system" cannot be implemented at the ports, but by adapting MIA's best practices, each port should be able to conduct passenger screening operations more effectively based on its unique operational needs.

We consider CBP's ongoing action responsive to the recommendation; the recommendation is now resolved. The recommendation will remain open until we receive and review support of (1) MIA's best practices for using the Targeting Framework and (2) how the ports have adapted it to meet their specific operational requirements for passenger screening.

Management Comments to Recommendation # 2
Concur. The Office of Field Operations at Headquarters will disseminate guidance to all field offices and ports regarding retaining documentation when removing individuals from the biometric watchlist. The estimated completion date is September 30, 2015.

OIG Analysis

We consider CBP's ongoing action responsive to the recommendation; the recommendation is now resolved. However, the recommendation will remain open until we receive and review a copy of the retention documentation guidance when removing individuals from the biometric watchlist, and confirmation that it has been disseminated to all CBP field offices and ports.

Management Comments to Recommendation # 3
Concur. The CBP MIA Agriculture Air Cargo unit is currently reviewing and updating the following local Standard Operating Procedures for cargo shipments referred to USDA and for agriculture cargo safeguarding: 1) Cargo Shipments Referred to USDA, 2) Plant Protection and Quarantine 309 and Pest Delivery, 3) Agriculture Air Cargo Clearance, and 4) Agriculture Cargo Safeguarding Procedures. The estimated completion date is December 31, 2014.

OIG Analysis

We consider CBP's ongoing action responsive to the recommendation; the recommendation is now resolved. However, the recommendation will remain open until we receive and review a copy of each updated Standard Operating

Procedures: 1) Cargo Shipments Referred to USDA, 2) Plant Protection and Quarantine 309 and Pest Delivery, 3) Agriculture Air Cargo Clearance, and 4) Agriculture Cargo Safeguarding Procedures.

Management Comments to Recommendation # 4

Concur. The CBP Miami Seaport Anti-Terrorism Contraband Enforcement Team ATU will create local job aids covering: query building and hold procedures in the Automated Targeting System, and entering exam findings in the Cargo Enforcement Reporting and Tracking System. The Miami Seaport will also hold weekly ATU musters and ensure that muster logs are maintained for local records. The estimated completion date is January 31, 2015.

OIG Analysis

We consider CBP's ongoing action responsive to the recommendation; the recommendation is now resolved. However, the recommendation will remain open until we receive and review a copy of the local job aids for query building and hold procedures in the Automated Targeting System, and entering exam findings in the Cargo Enforcement Reporting and Tracking System.

Appendix A
Transmittal to Action Official

OFFICE OF INSPECTOR GENERAL
Department of Homeland Security

Washington, DC 20528 / www.oig.dhs.gov

DEC 18 2014

TO: Todd C. Owen
Assistant Commissioner
Office of Field Operations
U.S. Customs and Border Protection

FROM: Anne L. Richards
Assistant Inspector General for Audits

SUBJECT: *Inspection of U.S. Customs and Border Protection Miami Field Office Ports of Entry*, Report Number OIG-15-13

Attached for your action is our final report, *Inspection of U.S. Customs and Border Protection Miami Field Office Ports of Entry*. We incorporated the formal comments from U.S. Customs and Border Protection in the final report.

The report contains four recommendations aimed at improving passenger screening, agriculture safeguarding operations, and cargo targeting. Your office concurred with all of the recommendations. Based on information provided in your response to the draft report, we consider all the recommendations resolved and open. Once your office has fully implemented the recommendations, please submit a formal closeout request to us within 30 days so that we may close the recommendations. The memorandum should be accompanied by evidence of completion of agreed upon corrective actions and of the disposition of any monetary amounts.

Please email a signed PDF copy of all responses and closeout requests to OIGAuditsFollowup@oig.dhs.gov. Consistent with our responsibility under the *Inspector General Act*, we will provide copies of our report to appropriate congressional committees with oversight and appropriation responsibility over the Department of Homeland Security. We will post the report on our website for public dissemination.

Please call me with any questions, or your staff may contact Mark Bell, Deputy Assistant Inspector General for Audits, at (202) 254-4100.

Attachment

Appendix B
Scope and Methodology

The Department of Homeland Security (DHS) Office of Inspector General (OIG) was established by the *Homeland Security Act of 2002* (Public Law 107-296) by amendment to the *Inspector General Act of 1978*. This is one of a series of audit, inspection, and special reports prepared as part of our oversight responsibilities to promote economy, efficiency, and effectiveness within the Department.

We conducted this inspection to determine whether selected Miami Field Office ports of entry operations comply with CBP's policies and procedures. The scope of this inspection was limited to operations in FYs 2011–13 at selected Miami Field Office ports of entry. We identified and selected the Miami Field Office ports of entry with the largest volume of passengers and cargo, resulting in review of operations at MIA, Miami Seaport, and Port Everglades (air and sea). We judgmentally selected operations within CBP's Office of Field Operations areas of responsibility as depicted below:

Passenger Screening
- Passenger Analytical Units
- Biometrics Watchlist
  - Promotions
  - Demotions

Cargo Targeting
- Cargo Targeting (Sea)
- High Security Bolt Seals

Agriculture Safeguarding
- Pest Exclusion for Cut Flowers

Fines, Penalties, and Forfeiture
- Seized Asset Management

We obtained and analyzed national and local policies and procedures for each operation selected. We reviewed prior OIG and U.S. Government Accountability Office reports. We interviewed officials from CBP's Office of Field Operations at headquarters, officials at the Miami Field Office, and officials at each selected port of entry. We also observed selected operations at the ports. We identified and performed tests of controls over the operations, except for passenger screening operations, because it was not feasible. We conducted limited testing on data obtained from CBP to determine data validity and reliability. We did not rely on the data to make any significant conclusions in the report. We developed findings and recommendations based on the results of our testing and other observations.

Sampling Methodology for Each Area

Cargo Targeting

We drew a statistical sample of 381 medium- to high-risk shipments to test for compliance with applicable policies and procedures.[2] We used IDEA software to randomly select the 381 shipments from the population of medium and high-risk shipments that arrived at Miami Seaport or Port Everglades from FYs 2011 to 2013.

To address our objective for cargo targeting operations, we determined whether Miami Seaport and Port Everglades cargo targeting operations complied with the CBP *National Maritime Targeting Policy 3290-007 B*, December 28, 2008. We obtained a population of 50,076 medium- to high-risk shipments for FYs 2011–13.

Based on CBP's *National Maritime Targeting Policy*, we reviewed shipments in the Automated Targeting System to determine if they received the appropriate level of review, hold, and/or exam. If shipments that required an examination did not receive it, we reviewed the shipment to determine whether the exam was waived, or if it met the standard exception requirements. If an anomaly was found during a Non-Intrusive Inspection, we reviewed the shipment to determine if it was referred for a physical examination. Lastly, we reviewed examined shipments to determine if all examination findings were entered into the Automated Targeting System.

Table 1: Shipment Characteristics of the Population

	Number of Samples	Sample Percentage	Population-wide Compliance or Noncompliance Based on Sampled Inference
Compliant with Guidance	377	99%	49,575
Not Compliant with Guidance	4	1%	501
Total	**381**	**100%**	**50,076**

Source: DHS OIG review of automated targeting data.

High Security Bolt Seals

We drew a statistical sample of 384 high security bolt seal records to test for compliance with applicable Miami Field Office policies and procedures.[3] We used IDEA software to randomly select the 384 bolt seals from the population

---

[2] Given a population size of 50,076 medium- to high-risk shipments, a 95 percent confidence level, 5 percent sampling error, and 50 percent population proportion, a random sample would total 381.

[3] Given a population size of 409,650 high security bolt seals, a 95 percent confidence level, 5 percent sampling error, and 50 percent population proportion, a random sample would total 384.

of bolt seals that were affixed to sea cargo containers at Miami Seaport and Port Everglades during FYs 2011–13.

To address our objective for cargo targeting operations, we reviewed a population of 409,650 high security bolt seals to determine whether the Miami Seaport and Port Everglades complied with the *CBP's Seal Standards* and other applicable policies and procedures.

Based on *CBP's Seal Standards*, we conducted a review to determine if the Miami Field Office bolt seal coordinator's inventory records had the required fields. We also reviewed to determine whether port supervisory inventory records and CBP officer inventory records had required fields as specified in the bolt seal policy. We further reviewed port of entry records to determine compliance with inoperable/unusable bolt seal policies and lost or stolen bolt seal policies. In addition, we reviewed CBP's Cargo Enforcement Reporting and Tracking System records to determine whether the ports of entry were properly recording bolt seal information.

Based on our review of the Miami Field Office's bolt seals operations, we are able to infer the following characteristics of the total population. See table 2.

Table 2: Bolt Seal Characteristics of the Population

	Number of Samples	Sample Percentage	Population-wide Compliance or Noncompliance Based on Sampled Inference
Compliant with Guidance	142	37%	151,485
Not Compliant with Guidance	242	63%	258,165
Total	**384**	**100%**	**409,650**

Source: DHS OIG review of bolt seal compliance.

Agriculture Safeguarding

For pest exclusion for cut flowers, we selected a random statistical sample of 378 actionable pests for cut flower cases for FYs 2011–13 for pest exclusion. We conducted our sample at MIA.

Based on our review of MIA's *Agriculture Cargo Safeguarding* and MIA's *Cargo Shipment Referrals to the United States Department of Agriculture,* we reviewed whether CBP referred the pest to USDA, and whether the shipment was safeguarded. We also reviewed whether CBP identified the cargo shipment containing the pest and whether complete contract information was included, such as the address and phone number of the owner/consignee of the commodity. Lastly, we reviewed whether CBP clearly noted which action was required by the shipper (treated, destroyed, or re-exported) and whether the pest case was closed.

We drew a statistical sample based on a 95-percent confidence level, given a population of 24,023, a 5 percent sampling error, and a 50 percent population proportion. We did not report the results of noncompliance for this area because noncompliance was based on outdated MIA policies and procedures. However, MIA adhered to the required process outlined in USDA's *Manual for Agriculture Clearance* and USDA's *Emergency Action Notification (EAN) v2.0 Policy Guide.*

Fines, Penalties, and Forfeiture

For seized asset management, we drew a judgmental sample of 101 seizure cases to review for compliance with applicable Miami Field Office policies and procedures. We selected the first 101 seizure cases from the population of seizures conducted at the Miami Field Office from FYs 2011 to 2013. However, the Miami Field Office's Fines, Penalties, and Forfeiture office could not locate 5 of the 101 files. We tested the remaining 96 files for compliance with CBP policies and procedures. Not all tests of controls were applicable for each of the 96 cases reviewed.

To address our objective for seizure asset management, we reviewed seizure cases to determine whether the Miami Field Office complied with CBP's *Seized Asset Management and Enforcement Procedures Handbook (HB 4400-01A and HB 4400-01B).*

We reviewed the seizure case file to determine, when applicable, whether seized property was transferred, a Notice of Seizure was issued, and whether Currency/Monetary Instruments were deposited, within the required timeframes. We tested to determine whether information in the Seized Asset and Case Tracking System agreed with information from documents in the seized property file. We also reviewed whether the Notice of Seizure included the appraised value of seized property as well as an original signature, and whether the Notice of Intent to Forfeit met the minimum requirements. Lastly, we reviewed whether adequate documentation existed for onsite mitigation and for disposition of seized property.

For compliance testing for held property, out of 37,754 seizure cases, we judgmentally selected 29 case files identified as having held property in the permanent storage facility. At the time we visited the facility, 15 of the 29 were currently held there because others had been transferred or disposed.

We visited the permanent storage facility and reviewed the held property to ensure that the information on the DHS Form 6051 attached to the seized property matched the information in CBP's Seized Asset and Case Tracking System and DHS Form 6051 on file.

Our field work was conducted between September 2013 and May 2014. We conducted this review under the authority of the *Inspector General Act of 1978*, as amended, and according to the Quality Standards for Inspection and Evaluation, issued by the Council of the Inspectors General on Integrity and Efficiency.

Appendix C
CBP Comments to the Draft Report

1300 Pennsylvania Avenue NW
Washington, DC 20229

**U.S. Customs and
Border Protection**

NOV 1 4 2014

MEMORANDUM FOR: Anne L. Richards
Assistant Inspector General for Audits
Department of Homeland Security

FROM: Eugene H. Schied
Assistant Commissioner
Office of Administration

SUBJECT: Response to OIG Draft Report "Inspection of U.S. Customs and
Border Protection Miami Field Office Ports of Entry"

We appreciate the opportunity to review and provide comments on the Office of Inspector
General's (OIG) draft report entitled, "Inspection of U.S. Customs and Border Protection (CBP)
Miami Field Office Ports of Entry," (13-149-AUD-CBP).

In the draft report OIG recognized as a best practice CBP/Office of Field Operations (OFO)
Miami International Airport's (MIA) effective leverage of CBP systems to track passengers who
have records for violations of laws or for other significant events. OIG acknowledged CBP/OFO
Miami Field Office (MFO) complied with existing national CBP policies and procedures. And
OIG found only minor deficiencies in MFO's operations for cargo targeting and seized asset
management.

The draft report contained four recommendations addressed to the CBP/OFO/MFO Director of
Field Operations. Please see below for the specific OIG recommendations, as well as CBP's
response and corrective action plans to implement each assigned recommendation.

Recommendation 1: We recommend that the CBP Miami Field Office, Director of Field
Operations: Share the best practices of MIA's use of the Targeting Framework and allow ports
to use those aspects that may be most beneficial to their unique operational needs, until the CBP
MFO obtains a system to effectively document, monitor, and report on passenger screening
operations.

CBP Response: Concur. CBP already has systems in place that are used to document, monitor
and report on passenger screening operations. MIA uses the Targeting Framework, which is
available to all ports of entry nationwide, as an additional tool. MIA has leveraged the Targeting
Framework's capabilities to track lookouts and significant events. The use of the Targeting
Framework is effective for MIA, but may not be effective for other ports because each port has
unique needs for tracking targets from initial identification to final disposition. For some ports
that do not have a dedicated cadre of officers in a Command Center environment, the Targeting
Framework would prove burdensome.

15

OIG Draft Report - Inspection of CBP Miami POEs
Page 2

The Miami Field Office will share the best practices of MIA's use of the Targeting Framework and allow ports to use those aspects which may be most beneficial to their unique operational needs. The Miami Field Office will promote the best practices of the existing Targeting Framework capabilities for ports to adapt based on their operational requirements.

Estimated Completion Date: January 31, 2015

Recommendation 2: We recommend that the CBP Miami Field Office, Director of Field Operations: Develop a retention policy for documentation when removing individuals from the biometric watchlist.

CBP Response: Concur. Further discussions with the OIG determined the recommendation will be addressed to the Assistant Commissioner, OFO. OFO-Headquarters will disseminate guidance to all field offices and ports regarding retaining documentation when removing individuals from the biometric watchlist.

Estimated Completion Date: September 30, 2015.

Recommendation 3: We recommend that the CBP Miami Field Office, Director of Field Operations: Review and update policies and procedures for cargo shipments referred to USDA and for agriculture cargo safeguarding to properly reflect current practices and procedures.

CBP Response: Concur. The MIA Agriculture Air Cargo unit is currently reviewing and updating the following local Standard Operating Procedures (SOP) for cargo shipments referred to U.S. Department of Agriculture (USDA) and for agriculture cargo safeguarding: 1) Cargo Shipments Referred to USDA, 2) Plant Protection and Quarantine (PPQ) 309 and Pest Delivery, 3) Agriculture Air Cargo Clearance, and 4) Agriculture Cargo Safeguarding Procedures.

Estimated Completion Date: December 31, 2014

Recommendation 4: We recommend that the CBP Miami Field Office, Director of Field Operations: Develop job aids and hold musters as refresher training for Advance Targeting Unit (ATU) employees.

CBP Response: Concur. The Miami Seaport (MSE) Anti-Terrorism Contraband Enforcement Team (A-TCET) ATU will create local Job Aids covering: query building in Automated Targeting System (ATS), hold procedures in ATS, and entering exam findings in the Cargo Enforcement Reporting and Tracking System (CERTS). The MSE will also hold weekly ATU musters and ensure that muster logs are maintained for local records.

Estimated Completion Date: January 31, 2015

Again, thank you for the opportunity to review and comment on this draft report. Technical and sensitivity comments were previously provided under separate cover. We look forward to working with OIG on future homeland security issues. If you have questions or require additional information please contact me at (202) 344-2300, or have a member of your staff contact Ms. Kathryn Dapkins, Component Audit Liaison, Management Inspections Division at (202) 325-7732.

Appendix D
Office of Audits Major Contributors to This Report

Paul H. Wood, Director
Maryann Pereira, Audit Manager
April E. Evans, Program Analyst
Nick Jathar, Auditor
Armando Lastra, Auditor
Marissa Weinshel, Program Analyst
Hortencia Francis, Program Analyst
Islam Muhammad, Ph.D., Statistician
Kevin Dolloson, Communications Analyst
Erica Stern, Independent Referencer
Phillip Emswiler, Independent Referencer

Appendix E
Report Distribution

Department of Homeland Security

Secretary
Deputy Secretary
Chief of Staff
Deputy Chief of Staff
General Counsel
Director, GAO/OIG Liaison Office
Assistant Secretary for Office of Policy
Assistant Secretary for Office of Public Affairs
Assistant Secretary for Office of Legislative Affairs
CBP Audit Liaison

Office of Management and Budget

Chief, Homeland Security Branch
DHS OIG Budget Examiner

Congress

Congressional Oversight and Appropriations Committees

ADDITIONAL INFORMATION AND COPIES

To view this and any of our other reports, please visit our website at: www.oig.dhs.gov.

For further information or questions, please contact Office of Inspector General Public Affairs at: DHS-OIG.OfficePublicAffairs@oig.dhs.gov. Follow us on Twitter at: @dhsoig.

www.ingramcontent.com/pod-product-compliance
Lightning Source LLC
Chambersburg PA
CBHW081145280526
45787CB00007B/3230